FIFTY
FASHION
DESIGNERS
THAT
CHANGED
THE
WORLD

DESIGN MUSEUM

FIFTY FASHION DESIGNERS

THAT CHANGED THE WORLD

LAUREN COCHRANE

conran
OCTOPUS

FIFTY
FASHION
DESIGNERS

FIFTY
FASHION
DESIGNERS

The impact of fashion design on our day-to-day lives is undeniable – what we put on our bodies in the morning helps present an image to the world. But rarely do we think about who is behind the design of that black blazer that makes us walk tall into a meeting, or the dreamy strapless gown that adds an edge of bygone glamour to the present day. This is a book that pays tribute to the designers who have helped create the clothes we wear – and love – and changed the fashion world into the one we recognize. It's an attempt to tell the story of how each designer has changed their world and – more often than not – ours as well.

Some of the names here – Ralph Lauren, Alexander McQueen, Coco Chanel – are well known. Some – Gaby Aghion, Patrick Kelly, Claire McCardell – are less so. All, however, have produced something unique, something new and something relevant – either through their influence on other designers (see Madame Grès) or through their ability to express the current moment (the likes of Christopher Kane and Alexander Wang). While fashion, of course, boasts far more than 50 significant and important names in its recent history, this is, we hope, a very good place to start.

From full-skirted frocks to elegant coats – and more outlandish creations – fashion over the last 100 years has provided some looks to remember. Presented everywhere from brasseries to boulevards, there is a world of creativity to explore. Sit down and enjoy.

The women whom Jeanne Lanvin (1867–1946) dressed have her daughter to thank. Lanvin was happily crafting out a career as a milliner until Marguerite was born in 1897. It was then that she began making clothes for her little girl. Womenswear followed when her millinery clients began asking for copies.

This happy mother–daughter union was central to the Lanvin brand and can be seen in the logo based on a 1907 picture of the two, first seen in 1954. It speaks volumes about the kind of designer that the Breton-born Lanvin was – femininity was central to what she made, the glow of youth a fascination.

Lanvin joined the Chambre syndicale de la haute couture parisienne (the fashion trade union) and unapologetically set about designing feminine clothes. These included full-skirted *robes de style*, picture dresses with rich embroidery, and pyjamas influenced by Eastern dress. A pretty, powdery blue that Lanvin spotted in a Fra Angelico painting became the brand's shade, one that remains in use on Lanvin packaging.

Lanvin's pre-war formula of clothes made for romance was irresistible. Demand grew through the 1920s, with seven stores opening internationally and a workforce of 1,200. Film stars including Mary Pickford wore her clothes, and American women in particular flocked to buy each collection. As well as being creative, Lanvin was a smart businesswoman, setting up her own dyeworks and launching fragrances alongside sport and lingerie collections.

Lanvin died in 1946 but the current creative director of her house, the Israeli fashion designer Alber Elbaz, is a worthy successor. He has been designing Lanvin collections since 2001. Feminine, luxurious clothes are his métier, but his masterstroke is keeping the Lanvin romance distinctly modern.

Mother and daughter were the principal characters of the Lanvin story, and matching designs like these show this in action. Pretty and feminine, and worn with coordinating accessories, the Lanvin picture dress design was suitable for all ages, and years ahead of its time.

COCO CHANEL

Gabrielle 'Coco' Chanel (1883–1971) is a giant of 20th-century fashion – a bona fide household name. At the height of her powers in the 1920s and 1930s, the designer pioneered everything from the 'little black dress' to ropes of pearls, Breton tops, handbags with gilt chains, designer perfumes, mannish trousers and, of course, what is now referred to as the Chanel suit.

Chanel had little patience for fantasy in fashion. Instead, she declared that she had 'freed the body', doing away with the corsets that women wore. She opened her first shops between 1913 and 1915, selling simple jersey dresses, but she had to wait almost ten years before the advent of the flapper meant that the rest of the world caught up with her ideas. Chanel became the designer to dress this generation of bright young things. Her LBD, bob and string of pearls are now synonymous with the 1920s.

The designer closed her house at the outbreak of war in 1939. By this time, she boasted a famous boutique at 31, rue Cambon in Paris, a recognizable double 'C' logo and the perfume Chanel No. 5, which made her one of the world's richest designers. Her comeback into clothes in 1954 may have contrasted with the ultra-feminine 1950s shapes, but the tweed suit, gilt-chained handbag and pearls went on to become the last word in chic, elegant clothing. It is these house codes that Karl Lagerfeld has so successfully woven into his own work for Chanel. Creative director since 1983, Lagerfeld has ensured that Coco's spirit lives on.

Right: Bathed in Mediterranean sunlight, wearing sporty stripes and trademark pearls, a young Coco Chanel smiles, and so she should. She was always the best advertisement for her own designs and remained a figure of simple chic.

Below: A little black dress, dressed up with yards of pearls was a later uniform.

MADELEINE VIONNET

The contemporary concept of 'hanger appeal' had no place in Madeleine Vionnet's world. The designer began working in fashion as a child in the 1880s and reached the height of her fame in the early 1930s. She made clothes that may have looked unremarkable before the wearer put them on but, with a body inside them, they came alive. Women like Josephine Baker and Jean Harlow could testify to their magic.

The French-born Madeleine Vionnet (1876–1975) founded her house in 1912. She will be forever associated with the bias cut – cutting fabric on the diagonal for a fluid line. Inspired by classical drapery, she modernized it for a 1930s audience. Her floor-length designs were often made from one piece of fabric – jersey and satin were favourites – that skimmed the wearer's body for optimum elegance.

Simplicity was everything. Vionnet shunned corsets, and her clothes – unlike the majority around at the time – had few fastenings. The seeming effortlessness belied the hard work that went on behind the scenes; these dresses were feats of construction, with Vionnet working rather like an engineer. Instead of sketching, she often first trialled her dresses on small, doll-like dummies before scaling them up.

Vionnet shut the doors to her house in 1939, at the outbreak of the Second World War. It was relaunched in 2006, and six years later Kazakhstani businesswoman Goga Ashkenazi bought a majority stake. Hussein Chalayan now designs the demi-couture collection, but Vionnet's legacy goes beyond this. Designers ranging from Karl Lagerfeld to Dries Van Noten have paid homage to her modern classicism.

This magazine cover from 1934 isn't just a striking image – it's the perfect backdrop to show off Vionnet's signature gown. Consummately draped, so as to skim the wearer's curves, it is the picture of 1930s style, with the qualities that typified Vionnet's designs: sleek, elegant and womanly.

VOTRE BEAUTÉ

4 frs.

SEPTEMBRE 1934
23e ANNÉE - N° 298
PUBLICATION MENSUELLE

MODÈLE DE VIONNET
PHOTO MEERSON

Soyez belle, on vous épie...

CLAIRE McCARDELL

During the 1940s, when Claire McCardell (1905–58) was designing clothes, the concept of American sportswear was far from defined – if it was even a concept at all. Paris still dictated trends, and a romantic idea of femininity dominated. McCardell's work was different, and distinctly American. It was functional design for active women.

McCardell, who was born in Maryland, launched her label in 1940 after working with fellow American designer Hattie Carnegie. While she shared an appreciation of clean lines and no-nonsense fashion with Carnegie, McCardell's own work added an almost tomboyish aspect. Her 'Monastic' dress, which she first designed in 1938, was pleated down the centre with only a soft fabric belt at the waist. Strikingly modern in its simplicity, it encouraged movement. The 'Popover' dress and her diaper bathing suit, both designed in 1942, continued this good work. With its wide sleeves and equally wide pockets, and priced at around $7 as a 'utility garment', the 'Popover' dress sold by the thousands. McCardell also pioneered the ballet flat as a fashion shoe, persuading dancewear company Capezio to produce a pump in 1944.

McCardell was at least 30 years ahead of her time and played a major part in starting an American fashion tradition. For this reason, US designers ranging from Calvin Klein to Marc Jacobs cite her as an influence.

Sportswear was Claire McCardell's world, and this shot, of a model enjoying the sun in a short jumpsuit looks bang up to date. This is appropriate enough, as McCardell has remained a reference for modern, active design into the 21st century.

MADAME GRÈS

Forever associated with gowns that brought a classical beauty to fashion through drapes, folds and pleats, Madame Grès (born Germaine Émilie Krebs; 1903–93) set up her first fashion house in the 1930s and dressed Marlene Dietrich and Greta Garbo. Famously working alone, she would painstakingly drape yards of fabric onto her client's body to create her signature designs, which turned modern starlets into Ancient Greek deities.

Madame Grès had originally wanted to be a sculptor and put this sensibility into her designs. She first worked under the name of Alix Barton, in partnership with fellow designer Julie Barton, and their clothes were immediately embraced by the fashion elite. After parting ways with Barton, Grès continued to design under the name of Alix. The draped gown was a consistent staple by 1937.

Grès emerged as the designer's chosen moniker – a partial anagram of her husband's Christian name, Serge – in 1942, after the war forced her to close the house of Alix two years earlier. She retained a devoted following of women who loved her artistic approach to clothes and her lifetime's quest to perfect a single gown. In 1967 *The New York Times* dubbed her atelier 'the most intellectual place in Europe to buy clothes'. Her influence persists decades after her death: designers ranging from Rick Owens to Haider Ackermann regularly pay homage.

Right: A Madame Grès fitting was, by all accounts, something to behold. Working directly with fabric, here the designer is seen in action, finessing one of her signature goddess gowns.

Below: Her own look featured a signature turban and, in all probability, a tape measure to hand at all times.

CHRISTIAN DIOR

Christian Dior (1905–57) made the year 1947 his own with what came to be known as the New Look. Doing away with the austerity of wartime, when fabric rations had forced a simple utilitarian slant on fashion, Dior's New Look was mannered and decadent. It accentuated the waist with the nipped-in 'Bar' jacket and used yards of fabric for full skirts that fell to mid-calf. The result was luxuriant and – as *Harper's Bazaar* editor-in-chief Carmel Snow proclaimed – a 'New Look'.

The influence of Dior's silhouette stretched over the next decade, too – the full skirts worn by American teenagers to rock'n'roll dances in the 1950s had their roots in Dior's designs. In high fashion, he became the last word in ladylike style, with elegant dove grey and lush bouquets of feminine flowers soon associated with the house. He dressed A-list names including Ava Gardner and the Duchess of Windsor and, by 1949, the house accounted for 75 per cent of France's fashion exports.

In the end, though, Dior's reign was short-lived – he died in 1957. By this time, he was an institution of French fashion. More than 2,500 people attended his funeral in Paris, and the route of the cortège was lined with flowers laid in tribute. He was succeeded at his company by the 21-year-old Yves Saint Laurent, and the Dior name has continued to exemplify of-the-moment French elegance. Raf Simons is the latest creative director. In place since 2012, Simons pays quiet tribute to the Dior legacy each season, while adding his own note of sharp modernity.

Dior quickly came to typify French elegance in the mid-century – as seen in this pretty pink gown cut to a New Look length, ladylike white gloves and bowed hat. It is certainly enough to charm the fisherman on the banks of the Seine, especially with the Eiffel Tower as a backdrop.

ELSA SCHIAPARELLI

It makes sense that Elsa Schiaparelli (1890–1973) was the great rival to Coco Chanel throughout the 1930s. The two women, and their approaches to fashion, could hardly have been more different. If Chanel was about streamlined, simple design, Schiaparelli's take was playful and artistic, often influenced by her artist friends, the Surrealists.

The daughter of an Italian aristocrat and born in a Roman palazzo, Schiaparelli was ahead of her time in her approach to fashion. One of her first designs in the 1920s was a sweater with a trompe-l'œil knit of a bow on it. The sweater was an immediate success and was the first in a long line of witty designs. She famously collaborated with artists – with Salvador Dalí on a hat that looked like a shoe, and with Jean Cocteau on embroidery for suits. Other innovations included bags that played a tune when you opened them, and an early example of a jumpsuit. She raised eyebrows in 1931 when she designed culottes for tennis player Lili de Alvarez to wear on court.

Schiaparelli worked hard to create a brand identity. She made shocking pink the colour of her brand and named a perfume after it. 'Shocking', launched in 1937, was the first perfume to come in a bottle designed to resemble a woman's body (in this case, Mae West's). It financed Schiaparelli's experiments in ready-to-wear, which she continued until 1954, when she retired. The Schiaparelli house relaunched its couture in 2014, with designer Marco Zanini as the creative director.

Nothing is what it seems in Schiaparelli's world. This model might have the gloves and sparkles of ladylike style but her hat – with its baseball cap design and peekaboo eyehole – adds that surreal element that is always at the heart of 'Schiap'.

HUBERT DE GIVENCHY

Audrey Hepburn's Holly Golightly character in the 1961 film *Breakfast at Tiffany's* has an enviable wardrobe, and the black dress she wears for the party scene is the jewel in the crown. It was the work of Hubert de Givenchy (1927–), the designer who worked with Hepburn throughout the 1950s and 1960s, honing an image that was all pared-back elegance and clean lines. Never flouncy and always exquisitely cut, Givenchy's clothes showed off its wearer, not the other way round.

A French aristocrat – technically a count – Givenchy founded his house in Paris in 1952 and by 1954 was dressing Hepburn in Oscar-winning costumes for *Sabrina*. Away from the silver screen, he was concocting other innovations. The 'Bettina' blouse – named in honour of model Bettina Graziani – was a man's shirt with frilled sleeves. Along with Cristóbal Balenciaga, Givenchy has been credited with designing the first sack dress, a shape that came to define high fashion in the late 1950s. Other women in the public eye were attracted to Givenchy's impeccable chic – Jackie Onassis was a fan.

Givenchy the label has continued to exist – although the man himself retired from fashion in 1995 – with designers Alexander McQueen, John Galliano and, currently, Riccardo Tisci at the helm. Hubert's influence is still powerful, however. A version of Hepburn's *Breakfast at Tiffany's* dress was auctioned for nearly £500,000 in 2006.

Right and below: The pairing of Givenchy and Hepburn was sublime, for work as well as play. Whether wearing a red dress for a dramatic entrance in 1957's *Funny Face*, or the perfect mac for an off-duty stroll along the Left Bank, she embodied the effortless chic of his designs.

GABY AGHION

Gaby Aghion's journey in fashion started simply – with six cotton dresses. The Egyptian émigré was living in Paris in the 1950s and keen to move beyond the confines of haute couture, to create something more immediate and better suited to the needs of the young stylish people she saw on the Parisian streets. Initially selling her dresses into local boutiques, she launched her label – Chloé – in 1952.

Aghion was a designer whose work was rooted in reality. Far ahead of her time, she made sure that her clothes didn't restrict women – ease of movement was crucial to her point of view, as was unfussy design that provided an effortless chic. Shapes were simple and often plain, she frequently used natural shades such as sand. Aghion, and Chloé, became fundamental to the growing ready-to-wear scene in the French capital, one that embraced an emerging, post-war consumer: the working woman on the go, with little time for endless couture fittings.

Gaby Aghion (1921–) herself fitted the type. First setting up her workshop in a maid's room above her flat, by 1953 she had gone into partnership with Jacques Lenoir, who ran the financial side of the business. The first Chloé fashion show took place three years later – at that most archetypal of Parisian venues, the Café de Flore on the boulevard St-Germain.

Aghion continued to run Chloé until the mid-1980s, and she boasts the distinction of having hired a young Karl Lagerfeld in the 1960s. The continued existence of Chloé, whose output has often been designed by women – previously Stella McCartney and Phoebe Philo, and currently Clare Waight Keller – shows that Aghion's idea of chic clothes that match their wearers' lives was right all along.

Brasserie Lipp in Paris is the appropriately Parisian venue for a Chloé fashion show. Showcasing the very French and feminine – but female-friendly – designs of Aghion, the models and most of the patrons seemed very happy to see them.

CRISTÓBAL BALENCIAGA

If the late 1950s and early 1960s are acknowledged as a period of architectural elegance in fashion, a large part of that is down to Cristóbal Balenciaga (1895–1972). A leader in his time, and still an influence today, his aesthetic was centred around silhouette and cut.

His most famous designs bear this out. Balenciaga gave the world the sack dress in 1956, a design that pre-empted the 1960s shifts by nearly a decade and feels wearable even now. Other innovations included block colours, which he introduced in the late 1950s, and wide dolman sleeves on jackets, which followed in the 1960s. Balenciaga was not interested in prettifying with unnecessary details. Instead, his clothes were often plain but sculptural. They put line and proportion first and framed women's bodies to beguiling effect.

Born near San Sebastian in Spain, Balenciaga showed his talent early: as a teenager he copied couture designs (his mother was a seamstress). He set up his tailoring studio in 1916, at the age of 21, and dressed members of the Spanish royal family. In 1937 he moved to Paris where he spent three decades as a much-lauded designer, finally retiring in 1968. Since his death in 1972, other designers have created collections in his name. The latest is Alexander Wang, the first American to design clothes for this revered European house.

Balenciaga's clients were often from high society. Here, Marella Agnelli – wife of the Fiat director Giovanni – is pictured in 1963 on the steps of a country house in Provence, perhaps the perfect environment for a Balenciaga gown. The vivid colour and subtle sculptural shape are set off just so.

YVES SAINT LAURENT

Tuxedos for women, the safari suit, thigh-high boots and the peasant blouse – some of Yves Saint Laurent's designs are nearly 50 years old but they continue to form the cornerstones of fashion as we know it.

His magic came from a knack for channelling streetwear into luxury fashion. He was a devoted champion of ready-to-wear. His Rive Gauche line was launched in 1966, taking inspiration from the likes of young women such as Loulou de la Falaise and Betty Catroux, to create clothes that suited youthful urban lifestyles. Yves Saint Laurent (1936–2008) always embraced the new: beatnik culture was an inspiration, and he used minority models on his catwalk from the 1960s onwards. He designed Catherine Deneuve's costumes for *Belle de Jour* in 1967, and Bianca Jagger's trouser suit in which she got married to Mick in 1971. Saint Laurent's muse was always glamorous but independent, able to stride forward on her own path.

The designer was born in Algeria and moved to Paris to study as a teenager. A precocious talent, at the age of 18 he won both the first and third prizes in the dress category of the 1954 International Wool Secretariat competition. Swiftly hired by Dior, he subsequently became the company's creative director at the age of 21, after Dior died in 1957. His own house followed four years later, with business partner Pierre Bergé in place. Notable moments include 1965's 'Mondrian' dress, based on the artist's abstract work; 1976's *Russian* collection, inspired by the Ballets Russes; and 1966's 'Le Smoking', a tuxedo designed for women.

The designer, who had consistently suffered from ill heath, retired from fashion in 2002 and died six years later. The house lives on, however, and is now in the hands of Hedi Slimane (see page 102).

Saint Laurent's mid-1960s collection of shift dresses, drawing on the neoplasticist paintings of Piet Mondrian, summed up the mood of new young consumers wanting something their parents wouldn't understand.

PIERRE CARDIN

Pierre Cardin's 1963 *Cosmocorp* collection was an unmistakably 1960s moment. This was, after all, a decade known for its 'youthquake' culture, where anything – even living in space – was a possibility worth designing for. Pierre Cardin (1922–) was one of several designers who did so – others included André Courrèges, Rudi Gernreich and Paco Rabanne. Cardin's USP was centred around simple, almost uniform shapes for both men and women in bright and bold fabrics, with graphic Op art patterns. Always future-thinking, he used the latest fabrics like PVC and nylon, and even invented his own, Cardine, in 1968. Unisex clothes, including tabards and cat suits, were promoted at his shows, along with cut-out dresses and miniskirts.

Cardin's imagination was honed early on. Born in Italy, he worked in fashion from the 1940s onwards, designing with Elsa Schiaparelli, and making costumes for Jean Cocteau's classic film *Beauty and the Beast* in 1946. After working with Christian Dior, he launched his own company in 1950, presenting his first couture collection in 1953, with women's ready-to-wear following in 1959.

Although this saw him expelled from the prestigious Chambre syndicale de la haute couture, it was a move that was in tune with the times. The democratization of fashion that came with the new decade suited the designer – he was able to design for a younger customer who could now afford his clothes. Speaking in 1969, Cardin argued that 'we are entering a world of tomorrow' and designed his collections accordingly. The designer's influence endures: Cardin's brand of futurism is regularly referenced on 21st-century catwalks.

Right: In a typical take on the space age, this advertising campaign shows Pierre Cardin marry cut-out shift shapes with sci-fi accessories fit for another dimension.

Below: His desire to live in the future influenced his interiors, too, judging by a 1971 shot of his studio.

BARBARA HULANICKI

Barbara Hulanicki's big break came in 1964 when a simple 25-shilling, pink gingham dress called 'The Barbara', designed for her fledgling label Biba, was featured in the British tabloid *Daily Mirror*. The style-hungry young women of 1960s London flocked to buy it – here was a design that suited the dolly-bird Mod of the time, but at a price they could afford.

Polish-born Hulanicki (1936–) based her Biba business, which she set up in partnership with her husband, Stephen Fitz-Simon, on the formula of cool, age-appropriate clothes at pocket-money prices. By the autumn of 1964 the first Biba store opened. It soon became a pit stop for the style icons of the era: model Twiggy and broadcaster Cathy McGowan, who presented pop TV show *Ready Steady Go!* Their fans followed and Biba fell victim to an outbreak of shoplifting. Hulanicki famously turned a blind eye, saying, 'When people are stealing, you're doing the right thing.'

Biba was the retail success story of 1960s Britain. A bigger store opened in 1966 to keep up with the demand, and the design of the clothes shifted with the kids coming into the store, moving from the sharp, graphic look of the early 1960s to psychedelic designs later in the decade. A deal to expand even further in the mid-1970s went sour and spelled the end of Biba but not of Hulanicki. She has reinvented herself as a successful interior designer, and her instinct for democratic style remains – she designed a range of clothes for Topshop in 2009, followed by one for British supermarket chain Asda in 2010.

This, the Biba store, wasn't just a shop – it was a mecca for young women on the hunt for clothes that signified their times and suited their pockets. An Op art jumpsuit worn with white ballet flats would have been just the thing to impress your friends.

MARY QUANT

Mary Quant (1934–) and the miniskirt will forever go together – in bringing hemlines up, the designer gave 1960s London its own look and created a style that women have worn ever since.

Quant's career in fashion began with Bazaar, the shop she opened on London's King's Road in 1955, in partnership with her husband, Alexander Plunket Greene. It was, Quant later said, an 'almost violent success' from the outset. Her designs, which were often influenced by the simplicity of children's clothes, frequently sold out, and she would have to make more in the evenings to ensure stock the next day. The miniskirt, or an early prototype of it, was first essayed in around 1958: Quant took it into the early 1960s, influenced by the designs of her French counterpart, André Courrèges.

The style suited the Chelsea set of young creatives of which the London-born Quant was part. She began designing when she was 21, rapidly ditching the restrictive, conservative clothes worn by her parents' generation. Her genius lay in an ability to pick up on the ideas and trends around her, and on the sheer joy of being young. She originally made the mini because 'the Chelsea girls had really terrific legs'. 'If I didn't make the clothes short enough,' she remembered, 'they would shorten them more.'

It took a decade in fashion for Quant to become a household name, but by 1965 her company was making over £7 million a year. She designed clothes for American department store chain JCPenney, and in 1966 released her autobiography, *Quant on Quant*. The same year, she launched a successful makeup line and received an OBE. And her outfit for the ceremony? A miniskirt, of course.

Mary Quant practised what she preached – she wore the miniskirt as well as designing it. At the height of her 1960s power, she modelled it perfectly. Wear with knee-high boots and five-point bob, and settle down at home to read the paper. An icon at rest.

LAURA ASHLEY

Now a name that conjures up floral interiors, the Laura Ashley brand has its roots in fashion. The 1970s was the heyday, when thousands of consumers bought into the rural nostalgia that ran through the smock dresses and Edwardian-style, floor-length pinafores. 'If you can make people feel like they're living in the country when they aren't, it's very helpful,' said Laura Ashley (1925–85) at the time, and she would eventually extend this aim to create an entire lifestyle.

The Laura Ashley company started humbly enough in 1953. Welsh-born Ashley and her husband, Bernard, initially sold head scarves and tea towels. The first successful clothing design was a gardening smock. Long floral dresses became a signature throughout the 1960s, even though they jarred with the dominant aesthetics of the time.

As the prevailing stylistic mood shifted from the futurism of the 1960s to the back-to-nature nostalgia of the 1970s, Laura Ashley fitted in perfectly. Her dresses weren't cheap but they were affordable for a growing urban middle class hankering after the country life. The first London shop opened in 1968, selling 4,000 dresses in a week alone. Expansion came quickly – Ashley opened stores in France and the United States. The very British floral designs, which were soon seen on furnishing fabrics, too, were an excellent export product. By 1975 sales had reached £5 million, and by the end of the decade there were 70 stores worldwide. While Ashley herself died in 1985, her formula of pastoral style remains popular today – more than 60 years after those first tea towels were sold.

Laura Ashley's aesthetic came with a nostalgia for an early 20th-century rural existence. Shots like this – often of the designer's family – formed a typical advertising campaign. With trademark pinafores and florals, and a backdrop of a fireplace, it is no wonder the company later branched out into interiors.

VALENTINO

In an interview for the 2008 documentary *Valentino: The Last Emperor*, Valentino (born Valentino Clemente Ludovicio Garavani; 1932–) was asked what women want. His reply was simple: 'They want to be beautiful.' Valentino has spent more than 55 years fulfilling this desire. Always championing elegant clean lines and couture-worthy details and finishing, the glamour and femininity of his dresses have a timeless appeal.

Born in northern Italy, he established his house – named simply Valentino – in Rome in 1959. The bold red dress, inspired by costumes Valentino had seen at the opera as a teenager, was a signature from the beginning. It was his 1962 collection, shown in Florence, that saw him gain international attention. With Giancarlo Giammetti in place as business partner the following year, the foundations were laid. Elizabeth Taylor was an early client.

Other A-list names came flocking throughout the 1960s – Jackie Kennedy wore Valentino for her 1968 wedding to Aristotle Onassis. Valentino's place as the favoured label for ladylike style in this decade of flux was assured. Always feminine – bows and lace became two other house codes – and forever tasteful, Valentino created a consistent demand.

The house continued to seduce into a new century – Julia Roberts wore a vintage Valentino gown to the Oscars in 2001. While Valentino retired from his house in 2007, he remains one of fashion's big personalities. Valentino creative directors Maria Grazia Chiuri and Pierpaolo Piccioli, meanwhile, have ensured that his house is the epitome of modern glamour.

Valentino is all about jetset, glamorous style. Walking with a barefoot, off-duty Jackie Onassis on the island of Capri, this moment says it all. Valentino is a designer who not only dresses the rich and famous, he hangs out with them during their downtime. A man in with the in-crowd.

OSSIE CLARK

David Hockney's famous 1971 painting *Mr and Mrs Clark and Percy* depicts designer Ossie Clark (1942–96) and his wife, the designer Celia Birtwell, in the artistic surroundings that have since become an integral part of his place in fashion history. Studying at London's Royal College of Art, Clark was classmates with designer Zandra Rhodes as well as with Hockney. He ruled London's bohemian fashion world from the mid-1960s to the early 1970s, reinventing the bias-cut shapes of the 1930s with a contemporary rock'n'roll edge and adding groupie-friendly pieces like cropped biker jackets and hot pants. Birtwell, meanwhile, designed the prints for his clothes.

First sold from influential shop Quorum on London's King's Road, Clark's clothes were worn by the It kids who walked down it. Some were Clark's friends, including the members of the Rolling Stones (he designed Mick Jagger's tour outfits in 1972), Jimi Hendrix, Marianne Faithfull and model Pattie Boyd. Clark became famous for his outlandish shows, which Birtwell has since described as 'happenings'.

Clark's work has been rediscovered since his death (he was murdered by his lover in 1996), with two retrospective exhibitions. Stella McCartney is just one designer who has acknowledged his influence, saying that Clark's strength lay in 'the perfect mix between sexuality and femininity'. It is these qualities that give his work power even today.

A young Charlotte Rampling with wild hair, an escapee from the city wrapped in an exquisite chiffon gown covered with poppies, could well have been the poster girl for Ossie Clark's louche, 1970s take on a very English romanticism. She is dressed for now, and whatever parties the evening might hold.

HALSTON

Sister Sledge's 1979 hit 'He's the Greatest Dancer' is classic disco and, aptly, Halston is namechecked in the lyrics as one of the fashion labels popular on the dance floor. Roy Halston Frowick (1932–90), who dispensed with both his first and last names when founding his brand, was the quintessential disco designer. A regular at Manhattan's Studio 54, he dressed the stars that went there, Bianca Jagger, Liza Minnelli and Elizabeth Taylor among them. They loved his simply cut but super-sexy designs. Using jersey crepe that skimmed the body, these dresses and jumpsuits had the requisite glamour but, crucially, did not restrict movement.

Originally a milliner, Halston designed the pillbox hat that Jackie Kennedy wore to her husband's inauguration as US president in 1961. He moved into clothes in the late 1960s and built up a client base that included Babe Paley and Catherine Deneuve. Halston became a celebrity in his own right in the 1970s. He was often photographed hanging out with Andy Warhol and the Jaggers.

Money came with fame. He made nearly $11 million between 1968 and 1973 and cashed in by selling his name to US conglomerate Norton Simons Inc. in 1973. The Halston name was licensed and it was soon spotted in closets beyond the A list's. This deal was, in the end, Halston's downfall. After various changes to the board, Halston was fired from his own company in 1984. Since his death in 1990, there have been various attempts to revive the label. The latest is Halston Heritage, which puts the 1970s at the heart of a commercial collection.

Halston was a designer and personality cult. Pictured here wearing trademark polo neck and side-parted hair, he is accessorized by two women in his draped, glamorous designs, as well as by a chic apartment – no wonder that everyone else wanted to be him.

DIANE VON FÜRSTENBERG 1976

The year 2014 marked the 40th anniversary of the wrap dress – the design with which Diane von Fürstenberg (1946–) first made her name back in 1974. A single piece of fabric with sleeves and a deep V neckline, all pulled together by a belt, the wrap dress is a typical DVF concept: sexy, flattering to all, but also highly functional. When explaining the appeal of the design to a journalist, von Fürstenberg once quipped: 'If you're trying to slip out without waking a sleeping man, zips are a nightmare.'

Belgian-born von Fürstenberg moved to New York with her new husband (a German prince) in the early 1970s and was soon deep in with the in-crowd of disco mecca Studio 54. Glamorous and connected, she launched her label in 1972, with a wrap skirt and shirt dress among her early designs. Diana Vreeland was a fan. The wrap dress, which followed two years later, put the two ideas together. It was an instant hit – by 1976 a million had been sold. The 26-year-old von Fürstenberg – wearing a wrap dress, of course – appeared on the cover of *Newsweek* the same year. The strapline called her 'the most marketable woman since Coco Chanel'.

The 1980s, a decade in which work trumped play, were a fallow period for von Fürstenberg. She relaunched the wrap dress in 1997, though, and hasn't looked back since. Her brand is now global and, as the president of the Council of Fashion Designers of America (CFDA), DVF herself is a symbol of American fashion.

DVF – as she is fondly known – wears her signature wrap dress for her cover-girl moment. It is her body language that says it all – this is a woman on the up, one not to be messed with. This is a statement that holds true nearly 40 years later.

Newsweek
March 22, 1976 / 75 cents
Rags & Riches
Dress
Designer
Diane von
Fürstenberg

STEPHEN SPROUSE

Famous for designing clothes for Blondie's Debbie Harry, Stephen Sprouse (1953–2004) was in the nucleus of New York's downtown milieu from the late 1970s. His clothes for Harry were typical of his output: an update on 1960s futurism with a punk-influenced colour palette of neon. Dresses were short and often featured an asymmetric hemline or a cut-out. In addition to Harry, his crowd numbered Andy Warhol, Steven Meisel and transgender model Teri Toye, who became Sprouse's muse.

Sprouse was born in Ohio and moved to New England to study fashion at the prestigious Rhode Island School of Design. He lasted three months, dropping out to work for Halston. He remained at the brand – the epitome of disco-friendly Manhattan chic in the mid-1970s – for three years, picking up on the Halston USP of glamour bordering on the decadent.

When he launched his own label in 1983, Sprouse added a streetwise element that made his clothes unique. His first collection featured a graffiti print on acidic colours, two elements that are very Sprouse. While his label was short-lived – it closed in 1988 – Sprouse continued to work in art and design as a freelancer. Recognition for his work came in 2000, when he collaborated with Marc Jacobs on a series of graffitied bags for Louis Vuitton. His early death in 2004 at the age of 50 ensured that the Sprouse name – and his pop-infused aesthetic – bleeped onto the radar of a new generation.

Stephen Sprouse had the perfect girl in the shape of Blondie's Debbie Harry. Wearing an asymmetric, graphic dress, with risqué side split, on the set of the video for 'Heart of Glass', she exuded glamour, beauty, cool and the edge of downtown.

JIL SANDER

Part of a wave of minimalist designers who came to prominence in the 1990s, Jil Sander (1943–) was the lone woman among the likes of Helmut Lang, Martin Margiela and Calvin Klein. Her designs were never girly but they were more empathetic to women's demands. She gained a reputation as a designer who made clothes – particularly trouser suits – that would make women feel elegant and confident at work. For the post-power-dressing decade, her workwear whispered rather than yelled.

Beginning as a fashion journalist, the German-born Sander set up her company in 1968 in Hamburg. She showed her collection in Milan in 1973, then Paris the following year, though with little success. Sander's story is a slow one, perhaps because it took time for fashion to catch up with the quiet radicalism of her designs. By the 1990s, however, it had. Sander's work in the decade was successful not only because she was part of a wider movement but because she belonged to the more approachable end of it. Rather than being austere, her clothes were refined – in both senses of the word.

By 1995 turnover stood at nearly £160 million and her clothes were sold into over 400 stores worldwide. Sander's company was bought by the Prada group in 1999, and then the trouble started. After wrangles with Prada CEO Patrizio Bertelli, Sander left the company months later. Returning briefly in 2003 for three seasons, and then again in 2012, only to leave in 2013, Sander is now believed to have retired. Both designer and brand, however, are still highly respected.

An advertisement for her own designs, Jil Sander created modern but subtly feminine workwear for modern women – like herself – throughout the 1980s and 1990s.

KATHARINE HAMNETT

The moment that Katharine Hamnett (1947–) met British prime minister Margaret Thatcher at Downing Street in 1984 is one that has gone down in both fashion and political history. Most famous for her straight-talking T-shirts emblazoned with political slogans, Hamnett created designs that were simple, utilitarian and aimed at young people primed for protest. The T-shirt she wore to meet the prime minister was typical and it contrasted sharply with the formal skirt suit Thatcher wore. Long and teamed with leggings and flats, it read '58% DON'T WANT PERSHING', referring to the US Pershing missiles stationed in Britain at the time.

The British designer, who studied at London's Central Saint Martins, launched her label in 1979 after freelancing for ten years. Clothes with a message were her calling card from the start – often oversized, with sportswear shapes and those graphic slogans, they chimed well with what was on the streets at the time. This was a decade that began, in the UK, with protests, demonstrations and strikes. Hamnett's idea was successful. She won the British Designer of the Year in 1984, and her designs were worn by UK groups Bananarama and Wham!

While the typography of her slogan T-shirt has been imitated for very different messages – first by the band Frankie Goes to Hollywood for their 'Relax' video and most recently in designer Henry Holland's rhyming T-shirts – Hamnett has remained devoted to creating simple designs that say essential things. A tireless campaigner, she has recently used her designs to campaign against fracking, overfishing and sweatshop tragedies, like the Bangladesh factory disaster in 2013. A formula, yes, but one that remains powerful more than 40 years on.

Right and below: Hamnett's Eighties slogans were style signposts of a politicised generation in the UK – worn by pop stars like Wham! on the television, and in Downing Street by Hamnett herself in 1984. Brave, uncompromising fashion with a message.

KENZO

To say Kenzo Takada (1939–) was determined to work in fashion is an understatement. The Japanese designer travelled from Japan to Paris by boat in 1965, spending six weeks on board. It was a journey that paid off. The designer set up his label, initially called Jungle Jap, in 1970, opening a store of the same name. He was soon one of the city's – and decade's – most exciting young designers, embracing ready-to-wear as the future of fashion.

A contemporary of Yves Saint Laurent and Karl Lagerfeld, Takada used his Japanese heritage to give a point of difference to his designs. Cuts and shapes referenced the kimono and other traditional Japanese clothes, and in some collections he used the shapes of Japanese flowers. This segued into a theme of global cultures in his work – Peru, North America and Russia were all on Takada's mood board – and he boasted a catwalk cast that cut across races.

Kenzo's shows quickly became a hot ticket. By 1972, 2,000 people turned up to a show when only 500 had been invited. The label didn't just enjoy an insider following either – by 1980, Kenzo's turnover had reached nearly 20 million francs. This continued, bolstered by fragrances and a new business structure; turnover reached nearly 240 million francs in 1983. While Takada himself retired from the business in 1999, Kenzo collections are now designed by Humberto Leon and Carol Lim, the founders of New York label Opening Ceremony. Thanks to them, Kenzo has regained the kind of hip status its founder first imbued it with all those years ago.

Takada made it his mission to bring the aesthetics of all cultures and countries onto the catwalk. Middle Eastern and Mongolian dress was his preoccupation in the mid-1980s, with layered sweaters and hunting hats the charmingly eclectic result.

RALPH LAUREN

Ralph Lauren's story is one in which the American Dream has proved a reality. Ralph Lauren – or, as he was born, Ralph Lifshitz (1939–) – began his journey in fashion with the humble neck tie. He started designing them in 1967, expanding the business with a $48,000 loan a year later. It was a gamble worth taking – Lauren's route to becoming a household name began in the 1970s.

He launched a line of men's shirts for women in 1971 and clothed characters in two major films – *The Great Gatsby* in 1974 and *Annie Hall* in 1977. An all-American look was honed and emerged fully fledged in the 1980s, when Ralph Lauren advertisements featured happy groups of wholesome, preppy men and women, often in an outdoor setting, and always wearing clothes that grandstanded 'American Culture'. He trades in American archetypes: the cowboy, the biker and the Hamptons sailor have all been part of his world.

Ralph Lauren was a pioneer of 360-degree branding, introducing homeware and furniture into his output early on. He has always been about inclusive luxury, and the Polo line – younger, more casual and with a lower price point – has been present from the beginning. Its polo-player logo is recognizable around the world, as are the shirts on which it appears.

Ralph Lauren is now a global name but his path to success could only be American. Neatly, much the same could be said of his designs.

Ralph Lauren loves the rough-and-tumble, out-on-the-open-range territory of the cowboy. A rugged flying jacket, Stetson hat and blue jeans make up his look for the ranch. Accessorized with a beat-up vehicle, trusty companion and the bluest of blue skies, it is certainly a lifestyle to buy into.

VIVIENNE WESTWOOD

Still designing in her seventies, Vivienne Westwood (1941–) will forever be associated with the beginnings of punk. With her then-husband Malcolm McLaren, she set up her shop Let It Rock in 1971, at the 'wrong' end of London's King's Road. It became the epicentre for the scene, with Westwood's designs – ripped T-shirts, with obscene slogans and bondage trousers – adopted as the uniform.

Westwood moved on swiftly to high fashion. Her Paris debut was with the *Buffalo Girls* collection of 1982. While its *Oliver Twist*-style mannerisms contrasted wildly with the work of other designers of the time, the collection gained recognition on an international stage. Her talent for mixing tailoring skills with a desire to push boundaries was plain to see. Other notable innovations have included the mini-crini, which turned the Victorian crinoline into a miniskirt, and the 'Rocking Horse' shoe, the wooden platforms first introduced in 1985.

Westwood received an OBE in 1992 – famously collecting it in an Eve costume with strategically placed fig leaf – and is approaching 'national treasure' territory in Britain. But the friction between tradition and punk-rock radicalism is part of the Westwood DNA. Now a Dame, she continues to rock the boat in collections designed with her husband, Andreas Kronthaler. Environmental issues are her current preoccupation. The Autumn/Winter 2014 show was inspired by a Peruvian tribe but, combined with the silhouettes of 19th-century couturier Charles Frederick Worth, the results were at once beautiful and unsettling – a hybrid that Westwood could, by now, surely trademark.

Tradition and experimentation are Vivienne Westwood's calling cards – ones she stays true to. Pictured here in her King's Road store in the mid-1980s, wearing a riding jacket, tweed skirt and those 'Rocking Horse' shoes, she neatly sums up her own brand in one outfit.

AZZEDINE ALAÏA

Azzedine Alaïa (1940–) started his clothing line in his own way. Born in Tunisia, Alaïa moved to Paris and designed clothes for exotic dancers at the Crazy Horse cabaret. He then worked for Thierry Mugler and Guy Laroche and was famously fired from Dior after only five days.

His first collection was shown in 1980 at his Paris apartment, reportedly with no music or even invitations. Even so, the fashion press crammed into the small space and fought over seats. This fervent response is now familiar to this designer who has had a cult following from the start.

The cult of Alaïa grew up around a distinct aesthetic from the get-go. With the nickname 'the king of cling', he advocated a body-conscious silhouette, from short, tight black dresses in stretch jersey to jewelled bustiers and leopard-print knits that covered the skin but left little to the imagination. Even leather pieces were sculpted around the female form, and he used zips around the body to gain the smoothest line.

With his designs worn by Alaïa's coterie of stars – from Naomi Campbell and Stephanie Seymour to Grace Jones and Tina Turner – the result was impossibly glamorous. His reign continued into the 1990s – Cher Horowitz, the fashion-inclined heroine of the 1995 film *Clueless*, even namechecks him as a 'totally important designer'.

Alaïa now refuses to show as part of the prescribed fashion season and delivers his clothes to stores on his own schedule. It is a testament to his talent – and the demand for his clothes – that the industry allows him to do so.

Right and below: The king of cling had his loyal subjects in the shape of supermodels. Everyone from Cindy Crawford to Naomi Campbell would be called in to model his clothes, on the catwalk and on the street. Campbell, here wearing a typically tight Alaïa creation, even called him 'Papa'.

PATRICK KELLY

Patrick Kelly (1954–90) had one aim with his clothes: he wanted them to make people smile. The designer, who first flourished in the 1980s club scene, was all about fashion that you could have a good time in. Dresses were often body-hugging and decorated with buttons (a Kelly obsession), while suits and accessories came in bold colours. Hearts, logos and Eiffel Towers featured liberally, creating an irreverent vision of 1980s glamour. Kelly was cool: Grace Jones and Isabella Rossellini wore his clothes.

Patrick Kelly was the life and soul of the party. His dresses – all multicoloured tulle and off-the-shoulder details – were made to have fun in. Kelly himself wore a contrasting uniform of dungarees and baseball cap – he let his designs do the talking.

He was far more than just a hedonist, though. Self-taught, he began working in fashion selling customized thrift finds in his native Mississippi. Later, while working unpaid as a window dresser in Yves Saint Laurent's Atlanta store, he met Saint Laurent's partner, Pierre Bergé. Bergé encouraged him to move to Paris, and Kelly didn't look back. By 1987 his clothes were on the catwalk, and his business had a turnover of nearly $7 million. The following year, Kelly gained the distinction of becoming the first black designer – and first American – to be accepted into the prestigious Chambre syndicale du prêt-à-porter, France's body for the ready-to-wear fashion industry.

Kelly's African-American identity was always present in his designs. One 1986 dress paid homage to Josephine Baker's banana dance, and Kelly famously handed out brooches of black dolls to clients. His runway shows were diverse, mixing models of all races and sizes. Although Kelly died in 1990 at the age of only 35, owing to complications from AIDS, he remains one of only a handful of black fashion designers to create a successful eponymous label.

CHRISTIAN LACROIX

1987

Christian Lacroix (1951–) is so intertwined with the 1980s that his clothes feature in one of the decade's era-defining books, Tom Wolfe's 1987 novel *The Bonfire of the Vanities*. Lacroix's dresses – opulent, extreme and very expensive – are worn by the Park Avenue socialites, the so-called 'social x-rays'. Rounded 'pouf' skirts and cropped, embroidered jackets were two Lacroix-isms. His was an aesthetic that revelled in vivid colours and maximal glamour.

Lacroix, who was born in Arles in southern France, was head of haute couture at Patou from 1981 and launched his own house six years later, after a £4.75-million investment from LVMH's Bernard Arnault. Mixing influences that ranged from traditional French and Spanish costume to the theatre, his collections were pure fantasy backed up by highly complex couture techniques. If designers like Armani dressed women for work, Lacroix provided their wardrobe for after dark. His name in the back of a jacket was an instant sign of status – Anna Wintour even put one of his jackets on the cover of her first issue of American *Vogue* in 1988.

Lacroix's fall from grace came as the recession of the early 1990s brought a more sober mood. He continued to show until 2009, when he staged his final couture show to an applauding fashion press. Since then, Lacroix has designed successful furniture ranges, and in 2013 he created a one-off collection for the relaunched Schiaparelli. His name remains much admired across the industry.

Opulent, glamorous and – some might say – over the top, Lacroix made dresses for dreams, and he was lauded for doing so. A standing ovation from catwalk models at his first couture show was only right. After all, who wouldn't want to wear one of these creations?

JEAN PAUL GAULTIER

If Gaultier's use of corsetry has its most famous example in the costumes made for Madonna's 'Blonde Ambition' tour in 1990, it is an interest that actually dates back to his childhood – the Parisian-born designer created his first corset for his teddy bear.

Jean Paul Gaultier (1952–) was a precocious young man, working for Pierre Cardin as a teenager and then for Jean Patou. He launched his own label in 1977, at the age of 25, but really made his mark in the 1980s. This was a decade where extreme creativity on the catwalk was as much a part of fashion as power dressing. Gaultier's underwear as outerwear became a trope. With this he mixed references to the London street style he saw on trips across the Channel, as well as adopting a playful approach to his own heritage: the Eiffel Tower and the Breton stripe have become Gaultier signatures.

As well as designing for performers such as Madonna and Kylie Minogue, and for films including *The Fifth Element*, Gaultier has enjoyed a parallel career as something of a celebrity. He appeared on *Eurotrash*, a late-night British TV show in the early 1990s, and released a record, 'How to Do That', in 1988. His fashion nous has been reassessed recently thanks to the exhibition *The Fashion World of Jean Paul Gaultier*. First staged in Montreal in 2011, it has now toured eight venues across the world and has had over a million visitors. In a new decade, it is Gaultier's designs that are once again in the limelight. The designer saw this as a moment to bow out on a high: he retired from ready-to-wear in September 2014.

A partnership that set the 1990s alight, Jean Paul Gaultier and Madonna were thick as thieves – two bottle blondes on a mission to sex up fashion. They did it with corsets complete with sequins and stripes. A designer and muse with a *soupçon* of ooh-la-la.

GIANNI VERSACE

The image of Gianni Versace (1946–97) surrounded by supermodels at the end of his catwalk show was a familiar one throughout the late 1980s and 1990s. It summed up the appeal of this designer. Glamour, beauty, glitz and fame were qualities that he channelled into his collections, and he created clothes that were meant to be noticed.

Versace, who was born in Calabria in southern Italy, began designing for brands including Genny and Callaghan in the 1970s. He went out on his own in 1978, drafting in brother Santo and sister Donatella to help him in the business. Versace's clothes chimed with the excesses of the 1980s. Short, body-hugging dresses in bright colours were a signature, with scarf prints and the increasingly recognizable Medusa logo central to collections. Anna Wintour, editor-in-chief of American *Vogue*, quipped that, 'Versace was always sort of the "mistress" to Armani's "wife".' The connection between Versace and sex appeal was sealed in 1994, when Elizabeth Hurley wore *that* revealing Versace safety-pin dress to a film premiere and became a celebrity overnight.

Although Versace was tragically murdered in 1997, his brand – now overseen by Donatella – remains a giant of Italian fashion, true to his formula of high glamour, sex appeal and couture-like finishing. With revenue in 2012 reaching €412 million, it is a formula that sells.

Right and below: Gianni Versace was a man adored by the rich, famous and beautiful. In life, he partied with the future first lady of France, Carla Bruni; and in death, fashion icons including Diana, Princess of Wales paid tribute. Glamour till the end.

GIORGIO ARMANI

Although he founded his label in 1970, Giorgio Armani (1934–) will forever be associated with the 1980s. His uniform – featuring a perfectly cut jacket, wide trousers and simple accessories – was the last word in chic for both men's and women's clothing throughout the decade.

Armani started as he meant to go on, providing the wardrobe for Richard Gere in 1980's *American Gigolo*. With clothes playing a central role in the plot (being put on and taken off), the film introduced the designer to an international audience. Armani's clothes were crucial to the power-dressing minimalism of the decade, when just wearing an Armani suit could gain you status in the boardroom. Armani also pioneered 'second' lines: Emporio Armani and, later, Armani Exchange were introduced for younger customers in search of something more casual.

Born in northern Italy, Armani briefly studied medicine and served in the army before settling on fashion as a career. His first job was as a window dresser at La Rinascente, a famous department store in Milan, and he freelanced for a number of Italian brands before setting up on his own. Even today, Armani's two shows – for his main line and for Emporio – remain highlights of Milan Fashion Week. He stays relevant by working with current style mavens like Lady Gaga – he designed the wardrobe for her 2012 tour. The numbers tell the story, too. Armani Group's annual revenue that same year was €2.1 billion.

Armani has perfected the suit for both men and women. In the 1980s his designs gave women the armour to wear into boardrooms but, as this advertising campaign shot by Peter Lindbergh shows, that is something that goes beyond decades. Tailoring, done the Armani way, is timeless.

ISSEY MIYAKE

If one aspect of 1980s fashion was all bodycon dressing and party frocks, the emergence of Japanese design on the international stage worked as as a counterpoint to that. Along with Rei Kawakubo, of Comme des Garçons, and Yohji Yamamoto, Issey Miyake (1938–) presented clothes that put concept over sex appeal, and function over glamour.

Miyake launched his label in 1970 in Tokyo, calling it the Miyake Design Studio. He showed his collection in Paris for the first time in 1973. Pushing boundaries of design, he told *The New Yorker* in 1983 that he wanted to 'find out what clothing might be'. In this search, he used paper instead of fabric and made unisex clothes. His Japanese heritage was present in clothes that alluded to the folds of origami or to samurai armour.

Miyake was also interested in clothes that could be worn by anyone, anywhere. His innovative Pleats Please line, introduced in 1993, addressed this concern, with tightly pleated designs that kept their shape under any circumstances. This was followed by A-POC (A Piece of Cloth), designs made from seamless fabric that a wearer can customize with scissors. These ideas were commercial as well as innovative. By 1997 it was estimated that 680,000 Pleats Please items had been sold.

Miyake, a survivor of the 1945 Hiroshima atomic explosion, remains a role model for non-Western designers aiming to succeed on the international stage. Although he retired from his label in 1999, he has successfully mentored younger Japanese designers, including Dai Fujiwara. He is now one of the directors of the Tokyo design museum 21_21 Design Sight.

In Issey Miyake's work, folds are used to great – and sometimes dramatic – effect. This shot of singer Grace Jones, in an Issey Miyake design, is a case in point. The famous contours of Jones's face are expertly framed by Miyake's graphic lines.

CALVIN KLEIN

'You want to know what comes between me and my Calvins? Nothing.' That was what Brooke Shields proclaimed in 1980, in an ad for Calvin Klein jeans. By this time, the designer in question was on first-name terms with his customers. His high-fashion concept of simple clothes influenced by men's tailoring got him featured on the cover of *Vogue*. And a more democratic approach saw his name appear on the pockets of jeans and the waistband of underwear. This dual strategy worked: after that ad, 200,000 pairs of Shields's jeans were sold in a week, and the underpants even became a storyline in the 1985 film *Back to the Future*.

The 1990s were just as good to Calvin Klein (1942–) as he developed his minimalism on the catwalk. Clothes were pared down to their essence – the shift dress was a signature, as were suits with simple cuts, worn by Manhattan's elite. Klein also continued to gain news headlines through advertising. A naked Kate Moss starred in ads for Obsession in 1993, and 1994's CK One – a fragrance for men and women – saw Moss again, this time in a clubby setting.

Klein, who was born in the Bronx, originally launched his brand in 1968 with a $10,000 loan. He sold it 35 years later in a deal worth $429 million in stocks and shares. Although no longer involved in the business, Klein – as a branding genius – certainly appreciates that his name still enjoys household status around the world. Designers Francisco Costa and Italo Zucchelli, who oversee the women's and men's collections respectively, have made sure that it has stayed relevant for a new generation.

Calvin Klein's advertisements summed up their era, as Brooke Shields showed in 1980, and Kate Moss in the 1990s. Moss wore his clothes off duty, too. Pictured here with Klein at a Costume Institute gala, she advertises the brand even when not in the ads. No wonder he looks so happy.

MARTIN MARGIELA

Launching his fashion house in 1989, Martin Margiela (1957–) became intertwined with the aesthetic of the 1990s. If 1980s fashion was all about glamour and excess, the decade that followed deconstructed these ideas and embraced a downbeat, intellectual look. Belgian-born Margiela, who had previously worked with the 1980s *enfant terrible* Jean Paul Gaultier, was at the vanguard of this change.

Self-referential collections were based around the construction of the clothes themselves rather than, say, a muse or a mood. Early on, Margiela exposed seams and questioned what luxury was by making clothes out of shopping bags and the white muslin used for toiles in couture ateliers. In place of the flashy label or logo, four white stitches sewn into the back of garments became the in-the-know signifier of a Margiela design.

Margiela's fashion shows often took place in unexpected places, ranging from the subway to the supermarket, and featured models cast from the street. The most famous example of the designer's questioning of fashion norms is his own insistence on anonymity. Interviews were answered by fax on behalf of 'the *maison*' and post-show bows were taken by the design team in identical lab coats. A photograph of Margiela himself was revealed, by *The New York Times*, only in 2008.

Despite his plans to circumvent a cult of personality, Margiela inevitably became an insiders' favourite, and from 1997 to 2003 he even designed for Hermès. The Maison Martin Margiela was bought by the Diesel Group in 2002, allowing for further expansion and stores. Margiela the man retired soon after, as an official statement confirmed in 2009.

What he is doing now is anyone's guess.

Anonymity is everything to Margiela, from the simple stitched labels at the back of his garments to the models on his catwalk. In 1995 the designer even put models in balaclavas, in a bid to make the audience question the concept of a fashion show and, perhaps, concentrate on the clothes alone.

MIUCCIA PRADA

Marc Jacobs called Miuccia Prada (1949–) 'the designer we all can't help watching', an accolade that expresses how much power Prada has over fashion now. In seven minutes – the average length of a fashion show – she has the ability to shape a season.

This has been the case for over 25 years. Prada inherited her eponymous business – which began, in 1913, with luggage – from her grandfather in the 1970s. She launched ready-to-wear in 1988, and the 1990s saw Prada's rise to the position she holds today: the most powerful female designer in fashion. Her longevity is largely down to her passion for remaining unpredictable. Her design process often begins with something she dislikes, and ends with her making something new from it. Resulting designs include the 'geek chic' collection of 1996, waders on the catwalk in 2009 and postcard prints in 2004. The introduction, in 1992, of Miu Miu – a secondary line, named after Prada's childhood nickname – only added to her influence.

If Prada has the ability to surprise fashion every season, some consistencies are evident. Socks and sandals are now a typically Prada combination, and among well-designed, wearable clothes an element of silliness – from the banana earrings of 2011 to hiking sandals covered in jewels for 2014 – provides an irreverence that is uniquely hers. This combination, and the business nous of Prada's husband, Patrizio Bertelli, have made Prada the brand a contemporary success story. Sales were up again in 2013 – rising 11 per cent – proving that intelligent, idiosyncratic fashion is something very much in demand.

Here's a setup that has become familiar. A coterie of supermodels, including Amber Valletta and Kirsty Hume, surround Miuccia Prada after the Spring/Summer 1997 show. Wearing layers of chiffon and flatform shoes, she is the leader of the pack – where she goes, womankind follows.

TOM FORD

In 1996, at the height of his reign rejuvenating Gucci, Tom Ford (1961–) declared himself a perfectionist. It is an observation that can be seen throughout the designer's career. Ford's look is not scruffy chic – it is polished, expensive and *almost* perfect.

The Texas-born Ford was first able to exercise his quest for perfection at Gucci, where he became creative director in 1994. The house was stuffy, irrelevant and on the brink of bankruptcy, but it was soon injected with Ford's other trademark – sex appeal. During his ten years at the helm, he introduced a 1970s-influenced louche glamour. Long jersey dresses with cutouts at the hip bone were memorable, and a Gucci velvet trouser suit was worn on the red carpet by starlet Gwyneth Paltrow.

Working with soon-to-be French *Vogue* editor Carine Roitfeld and photographer Mario Testino, Ford created advertising campaigns featuring smouldering, kohl-eyed models. The most notorious of these was for Spring/Summer 2003, where a model was shown revealing a Gucci 'G' shaved into her pubic hair. The adage that sex sells proved true. By the time Ford left the Gucci group in 2004, it was worth more than €2.5 billion.

Life for Ford post-Gucci has been almost as eventful. After a short hiatus, he launched his eponymous label with a fragrance and cosmetics. Menswear followed in 2006, and womenswear in 2010. He also fulfilled his dream of directing a film: *A Single Man* came out in 2009. Today Ford shows his collection at London Fashion Week, and his perfectionism – honed to a mix of nightlife glamour and super-luxe fabrics – remains a season highlight.

If anyone could invent a new erogenous zone, it is Tom Ford. While at Gucci, he zeroed in on the lower back, with jersey dresses that were slinky, sexy and a little bit louche. As such, they define Ford's world – one that remains seductive today.

REI KAWAKUBO

When describing her working practice to *Women's Wear Daily*, Rei Kawakubo (1942–) said: '[My] motivation has always been to create something new that didn't exist before.' This simple quest, with which Kawakubo has been engaged for some five decades, has kept her a place at the heart of avant-garde fashion.

The Japanese designer and her brand, Comme des Garçons, which was founded in 1969, hit the international fashion scene in the early 1980s. Along with other Japanese designers, such as Issey Miyake and Yohji Yamamoto, Kawakubo began to show her collections in Paris.

Comme des Garçons' first Paris show took place in 1981 and contrasted wildly with the contemporary idea of womenswear, which centred around glamour and girlishness. Using lots of black, distressed fabrics, shapeless garments and frayed hems, it was shockingly new – and, controversially, dubbed 'Hiroshima chic' by some critics. Her work was subsequently taken up by those in the wider creative industries; cult film-maker John Waters has described Kawakubo as his 'god'.

The designer's influence has only grown over the course of her career – as she continues to push boundaries, even into her seventies. Landmarks include the Spring/Summer 1997 collection, which featured dresses padded to distort the wearer's silhouette, and Odeur 53, a fragrance designed to smell like, among other things, burnt rubber. Her take on retail is equally innovative. A series of temporary 'guerrilla stores' has opened in unlikely locations across Europe since 2000, while her Dover Street Market stores in London, Tokyo and New York are the department store reimagined by one of the most unique minds in fashion.

One of fashion's greatest innovators, Rei Kawakubo questions everything about clothes. A landmark was Spring/Summer 1997, since known as the 'bump' collection. Doing away with the idea that women want to look streamlined, she added lumps and bumps deliberately. A contrarian of the highest order.

DRIES VAN NOTEN

Part of the so-called Antwerp Six who graduated from the city's Royal Academy of Fine Arts at the start of the 1980s, Dries Van Noten (1958–) showed the world that Belgian fashion was something to be excited about. Each of the Six was different: Ann Demeulemeester specialized in a punk minimalism, Walter Van Beirendonck played with Pop art, while Van Noten's name was associated with a discreet elegance that gained him a devoted following.

Van Noten had fashion in the blood – both his grandfather and father had stores in Antwerp, and he was taken to fashion shows as a child. He followed into the family tradition in 1989, when he opened his first store in his home city. His first men's ready-to-wear show took place in Paris in 1991, with womenswear following two years later. Van Noten now sells in over 400 places worldwide, despite never advertising. Once describing his aim as 'the idea of elegance without ostentation', customers flock to buy his carefully pitched clothes that are wearable but always with an edge of something interesting.

If his work in the 1990s had something of the deconstruction popular among Belgian designers of the time, a certain romance has emerged as a typical Van Noten theme. Using sumptuous fabrics and prints, his designs gently flatter women of all ages and body shapes. Van Noten's world is one without ego – the 2014 retrospective at the Paris Musée des arts décoratifs is a case in point. Rather than being a straightforward survey of his own work, the designer used the exhibition to explore his inspirations. The result was distinctly Van Noten: considered, magical, unmissable.

Using jewel-like colours, layered embellishment and easy, real-life shapes, Van Noten has stuck to his guns since the 1990s. These are clothes that are a pleasure to wear – just look at the serenity on the faces of this 1990s model army.

JOHN GALLIANO

While recent years have seen John Galliano's private life overshadow his work, his designs have been at the heart of fashion since the mid-1980s. Known for his dressing-up-box approach, he combines historical references and a flair for cutting. This worked for his own line and, from 1996 to 2011, for the house of Dior.

John Galliano (1960–) made his mark early on. Graduating from London's Central Saint Martins in 1984, his graduate collection, *Les Incroyables*, was influenced by clothes worn in the French Revolution era. It was bought by influential London boutique Browns and displayed in its windows. During the next few years his reputation continued to grow, with designs that included references to everything from 1940s gangsters to Victorian crinolines. A 1993 show in Paris, which featured Naomi Campbell and Christy Turlington modelling for free, was a turning point. It scored him orders and, after a short spell at Givenchy, landed him the job of head designer at Dior at the end of 1996.

Galliano revived Dior – sales tripled with him at the helm. Building on the founder's romantic temperament, he added fantasy. His shows featured a steam train, semi-naked supermodels in barely-there slip dresses and – notoriously – designs inspired by homeless people sleeping on the quays of the Seine. His post-show bow outfits became legendary, ranging from Napoleon Bonaparte to an astronaut.

By 2008 he was designing 19 collections a year, but in 2011 he came down to earth with a bump, when he was caught on tape using anti-Semitic language to diners in a café. Sacked from Dior, Galliano has since designed Kate Moss's wedding dress and worked with Oscar de la Renta. His latest role is as consultant to the Russian beauty chain L'Etoile.

Christian Dior couture was Galliano's playground. Modern romance in the late 1990s came in the shape of a deconstructed New Look, here worn with Masai neck rings. Jaw-dropping.

KARL LAGERFELD

Karl Lagerfeld (1933–) is enjoying his sixth decade in fashion. His image – black suit, gloves and tie, high-collared white shirt, pompadour and sunglasses – has made him so famous that his cat Choupette has her own Twitter account, with tens of thousands of followers. While Lagerfeld has his own label, his work for others is where his genius lies. 'My job,' he once said, 'is to bring out in people what they wouldn't dare do themselves.' The Hamburg-born designer started early. His CV boasts a stint at Balmain at the age of 17, followed by periods with Jean Patou, Krizia and Chloé. He was first hired by Fendi in 1965 and remains creative director.

It is with his work at Chanel from 1983, however, that Lagerfeld is most associated. When Lagerfeld took over, the house had already been consigned to history. His touch saw house codes like tweeds, double Cs and camellias reworked for the razzle-dazzle 1980s. Claudia Schiffer walked the runway in a short tweed skirt, bustier and open jacket, and Lagerfeld muse Inès de la Fressange wore an oversized jacket and matching costume jewellery, the very picture of power dressing.

Lagerfeld has managed to keep Chanel – and himself – relevant for three decades now. He does this by plugging into the zeitgeist. As picture-led digital media has grown, Chanel shows have increasingly adopted the 'wow' factor, with an iceberg appearing on the catwalk in 2010, and a Chanel supermarket, complete with fully stocked aisles and shopping trolleys, four years later. In 2000, asked what inspired him, Lagerfeld replied, 'Everything… there should only be one rule: eyes open!' It is this instinct that keeps him right at the top of the fashion tree.

The Lagerfeld look at its most iconic: sunglasses, gloves, and perfectly coiffed hair, inscrutable expression. The portrait of Coco Chanel in the background pays witty tribute to his career so far.

STELLA McCARTNEY

When Stella McCartney (1971–) was named Chloé's creative director in 1997, Karl Lagerfeld made a now-infamous remark. 'Chloé should have taken a big name,' he said. 'They did, but in music, not fashion.' As the daughter of a Beatle, McCartney has spent her entire career coming up against such scepticism and yet she has always managed to win through. McCartney's easy, flattering and real-life-friendly aesthetic is one that women love.

It is fair to say that the London-born, Sussex-raised McCartney was fast-tracked on to the fashion radar. For her graduate collection in 1995, Kate Moss and Naomi Campbell modelled. The Chloé appointment followed just two years later. McCartney's work there nodded to the house's chic 1970s heyday but added a sprinkle of Brit cheek to make it desirable for young streetwise women like her.

Her own label was launched in 2001, backed by what was then the Gucci Group. While her first collection took the humour too far for some critics, this was a minor niggle. McCartney's collections are now a favourite of smart women looking for clothes that will thrill but that will also integrate easily into busy lives. With evening dressing beyond the red carpet and well-cut trouser suits two of her strengths, the label earned £3.4 million in 2012. McCartney's ultimate vote of confidence came that same year when she designed the kits for the British team to wear at the London Olympics. The OBE she received soon after cemented her status as another McCartney of whom Britain could justly be proud.

A chic working mother with a need for stylish clothes that work in real life, Stella McCartney is basically her own customer. Unsurprisingly, her wardrobe consists of pretty much only her own clothes. She wears them well.

MARC JACOBS

Marc Jacobs (1963–) has been at the top of fashion's elite for over three decades now and shows no signs of fading from view. Soaking up the pop culture he is surrounded by, he combines it with a mischievous wit and an instinct for what women want to wear. The native New Yorker remains the ultimate zeitgeist designer – whatever the current zeitgeist happens to be.

Jacobs first made a splash as a 25-year-old wunderkind designing for preppy brand Perry Ellis. His now-infamous 1992 'grunge' collection channelled the street fashion of the time, but the downbeat clothes jarred with the all-American history of Ellis and he was promptly sacked. This did, however, provide him with a reputation as a new voice in fashion – one that arguably earned him the role, five years later, of artistic director at Louis Vuitton.

Jacobs held this role for 16 years, and the success of the collaboration became the blueprint for other old French fashion houses looking for rejuvenation. Under Jacobs's 'American in Paris' lens, the iconic Damier check was covered with the graffiti-like scrawls of designer Stephen Sprouse and dots from artist Yayoi Kusama, and everything from showgirls to bicycle couriers became inspiration. His Vuitton shows throughout the 2000s are burned on to the retina of recent front rows: trains pulled on to the catwalk, carousels spun, and elevators full of supermodels went up and down. Jacobs left Louis Vuitton in 2013 to concentrate on his eponymous line. Further success is a given.

A line-up of supermodels turned into nurses – in homage to a Richard Prince painting – was a highlight of Jacobs's 16-year reign at Louis Vuitton. Cool, cheeky but with desirable product always front row centre, it is a typically Jacobs conceit.

ALEXANDER McQUEEN

When Alexander McQueen (1969–2010) described the essence of British fashion as 'self-confident and fearless', he could have been talking about his own work. Awarded a Master's degree from Central Saint Martins in 1992, London-born McQueen became a symbol of a new era in the capital's fashion. Building on four years of apprenticeship on Savile Row, he combined technical know-how with a dark, cinematic look rich in historical references. Freelance stylist Isabella Blow, who was soon to start working at British *Vogue*, bought his graduate collection in its entirety. She became a crucial mentor for the young designer.

McQueen showed his first collection proper as part of London Fashion Week in 1993. His Autumn/Winter 1995 collection, entitled *Highland Rape*, featured models smeared with fake blood and wearing low-slung 'bumster' trousers, ensuring his reputation as the bad boy of British fashion. He was, however, also recognized for his talent: he was the creative director of Givenchy for five years from 1996; the Gucci Group (now Kering) acquired a majority stake in his label in 2000; and he was awarded a CBE in 2003.

The designer was instrumental in turning the fashion show into something truly spectacular – in 1998 amputee Aimee Mullins walked his runway on wooden legs, while in 2006 the show opened with a Kate Moss hologram. His show for his last collection, *Plato's Atlantis*, for Spring/Summer 2010, was one of the first fashion shows to be live-streamed.

McQueen committed suicide in 2010, at the age of just 40, but his legacy of rebellion and tradition remains. His right-hand woman, Sarah Burton, is now creative director, and it was she who designed the wedding dress that Catherine Middleton wore to marry Prince William in 2011. McQueen's work, celebrated in the 'Savage Beauty' retrospective at London's Victoria & Albert Museum in 2015, will no doubt go on to inspire new talent to push aesthetics to the darkest extremes.

Plato's Atlantis was classic McQueen: extreme shoes, fantastical hairdos and exquisite clothes that melded historical references with the cutting edge of digital printing. That this was his last collection makes it all the more poignant.

ALEXANDER WANG

Alexander Wang (1983–) is the wunderkind of contemporary fashion. He has made his name on a simple idea – creating a downtown, 'model off-duty' look that suits his crowd of native New Yorkers and also exports all around the world.

Wang, who was born in San Francisco, started early. He dropped out of New York design college Parsons in 2005, after creating a line of cashmere sweaters that appeared in American *Vogue*. His main line followed at New York Fashion Week in 2007 and quickly displayed his talent for mixing hip street and sportswear influences with a simplicity of design that women loved, whatever their personal style. A diffusion line – T by Alexander Wang – of jersey basics with that Wang twist was soon added, and his position as a leading exponent of contemporary cool was assured. By 2009 the turnover of the company was close to over $25 million.

It was Wang's appointment as creative director of Balenciaga in 2012 – when he was still only 28 – that showed he was being taken seriously by the fashion world. Now bringing his tough, urban aesthetic to the French house, Wang is part of the fashion aristocracy. He still does things in his approachable, commercial – and highly successful – way. In 2014 he produced a collection for high-street store H&M – the first American designer to do so.

Right and below: The young prince of fashion for the noughties – and still fresh-faced – Wang brings his easy, signature sportswear shapes to the catwalk. Worn with loose, laid-back plaits, models love them – like most Wang outfits, these are street-ready.

PHOEBE PHILO

When Phoebe Philo (1973–) returned to fashion in 2009, after a three-year break, there was a collective sigh of relief. Hers was a voice much missed in the industry – one that, throughout the noughties, had sung of clothes that were breathtakingly desirable but spurned fantasy in a quest for real-life luxury.

Philo is now the creative director at Parisian house Céline and, during her time at the helm, has made it the insider label to covet. She almost single-handedly pioneered a return to minimal, simple luxury, where feel and cut are paramount. An eye for the details of urban life adds just enough cool. Thanks to her, flat skater shoes became luxury items, and the check of a launderette bag gained new life as ready-to-wear with four-figure price tags.

Philo – who was born in Paris to British parents – began to make her impact on Parisian fashion in 1997, when she came to Chloé as first assistant to its new creative director, Stella McCartney. Philo took over four years later and gave Chloé its girlish 1970s-influenced aesthetic of wooden-blocked heels, smock dresses and bohemian touches. The 'Paddington' bag – one of her designs – was a huge hit. All 8,000 produced for Spring/Summer 2005 were sold before they even hit the stores. Nowadays, this reaction is one that Philo is accustomed to. Back in the driving seat of a French brand, she continues to create designs that prompt feverish desire.

Phoebe Philo's bow post-Céline show is a ritual for the fashion crowd each season. Always about simple elegance, she makes a grey sweater with hair tucked in, black slacks and Adidas trainers look the height of chic. Ours is not to reason why.

CHRISTOPHER KANE

Christopher Kane (1982–) is the kind of designer that comes along once in a generation – with a talent so undeniable that he fast-tracked his way to a spot at London Fashion Week straight out of university in 2006, at the age of 24. The collection, for Autumn/Winter 2007, was a series of short, neon-coloured lace dresses which were a breath of fresh air. Kane, who was already consulting for Versace at this point, became the poster boy for a cluster of London talent.

Kane's strength lies in his ability to marry an identifiable aesthetic with a hunger for something new each season – a way of thinking that chimes with our times. Since that debut, memorable collections have featured sugar-sweet gingham, open-mouthed gorillas, Frankenstein's monster and Princess Margaret. Constants include a love of industrial details (the seat-belt fastening is one of his house codes), a play between the dark and the sweet, and that neon palette. He once declared every other colour to be 'so banal'.

Working closely with his sister Tammy, Scottish-born Kane has created an impressive business, from tiny beginnings in an East London flat to an international name. Kane helped Versace relaunch younger line Versus in 2009, and in 2013 his company became the first British fashion brand to receive investment from a foreign company in over ten years. Kering, the parent company of Gucci and Balenciaga, is a majority shareholder. By extension, Kane is now an international fashion player.

A scrapbook of references comes as standard for a Christopher Kane show. London's leader of innovation turns the references into designs – often focusing on neglected classics – that women long to wear. It is thanks to him that the humble pool slide – featured on his catwalk in 2012 – enjoyed its renaissance in recent years.

CHRISTOPHER BAILEY

The appointment of Christopher Bailey (1971–) as creative director at Burberry in 2001 neatly began his reinvention of the British brand, making it relevant for a new decade. At the time, Burberry's luxury status was ailing, its much-imitated house check having become associated with 'chav' culture. The Yorkshire-born designer, who graduated from London's Royal College of Art and worked at Donna Karan and Gucci (under Tom Ford), reduced the check's presence to just 5 per cent of products.

Bailey's aesthetic is about tradition and modernity simultaneously. He uses the heritage of Burberry and turns it into designs that are desirable now. He has reworked the house's patented trench coat countless times, and British institutions from David Hockney to Jean Shrimpton have inspired collections. His success stems from an exacting mind that is as tuned to business as it is to design, and while at Burberry he has moved from creative director to CEO. His natural marketing skills show themselves in the brand's glossy, cool but classic campaigns. Celebrities from Sienna Miller to Romeo Beckham are featured, pristinely shot by Mario Testino. All this shows in sales – with total revenue standing at £1.3 billion in 2013.

The Burberry show is a jewel in the crown of London's fashion shows and is famous for championing British quirk. Bailey has made it rain on the catwalk, and pop star Paloma Faith played out the Autumn/Winter 2014 show. His early adoption of digital technology is also worth noting: in 2010 Burberry became the first fashion house to live-stream their show in 3-D. Bailey moves with the times, and Burberry does, too.

Given the multicoloured metallic treatment on the catwalk and as worn by Catherine Middleton, the patron of modern British tradition in the 21st century, the Burberry trench coat, under Bailey at Burberry, is the definition of a reworked classic.

HEDI SLIMANE

For the Parisian Hedi Slimane (1968–), fashion and music are two sides of the same coin. The designer, who is now creative director of Saint Laurent, has made music, and musicians' style, an essential part of his world since the early 1990s.

After designing menswear for Yves Saint Laurent in the 1990s, Slimane became creative director of Dior Homme in 2000, where he remained for seven years. Here, he transformed the label into the last word in rock'n'roll cool, with members of indie bands walking the catwalk, and bespoke music created by Slimane's musician friends Pete Doherty and Razorlight. Slimane's look – which was worn by men and women – featured a skinny silhouette, with subcultural influences to the fore.

Even though Slimane left Dior Homme in 2006, his influence remained. He worked as a photographer, documenting bands all over the world in a black-and-white reportage style. This came in use when he was rehired by Yves Saint Laurent in 2012 and was able to give the iconic French house a new, young energy from the start. He changed its name to Saint Laurent Paris, redesigned the logo and transplanted the design studio to Los Angeles, where he was then living.

Slimane's reboot of the brand has not been without its controversies but, much to the chagrin of naysayers, it has been successful. Collections that borrow from the rock classics chime with what consumers want. Sales in the first half of 2013 rose 14 per cent on the previous year. Rock'n'roll rebels with the budget to buy designer fashion are the demographic that Slimane owns.

Mixing art influence with classic rock'n'roll is a cocktail that Hedi Slimane concocts each season, tinkering with the recipe each time. His work at Saint Laurent seen here, all tight leather trousers and Purdy cut, embodies what we think of as cool now.

PAUL SMITH

In 2005 Paul Smith (1946–) described his aesthetic as 'tradition mixed with the unexpected' and this is certainly true when one studies his collections. The British designer, who had ambitions to be a cyclist as a young man, started working in fashion when he opened a shop in his native Nottingham, in the English Midlands, in 1970. He produced simple things – shirts, tweeds, jeans – but with just enough of a twist to make them into fashion items.

Introducing his first collection in 1976, Smith first came to real prominence in the 1980s as a sort of counterbalance to the flash mainstream culture of the time. His first London shop opened in Covent Garden in the late 1970s and sold quirky design objects along with clothes. It is this talent for retail that distinguishes Smith – he makes his stores destinations that transcend mere 'shopping'. This aspect has long appealed in Japan, where Smith has been successful since the mid-1980s and where he now has more than 200 outlets and concessions.

The 1990s saw Smith turn his attention to womenswear. His first women's collection debuted in 1993, providing another platform for his 'classic with a twist' brand identity. Updated tea dresses, tartan and tailoring have become trademarks, along with a joyful approach to colour. Smith now has 14 lines within his company and stores around the world. His logo – a scrawled signature – and iconic skinny, multicoloured stripes are globally recognized. It is all a long way from those Nottingham beginnings.

Will the real Paul Smith please stand up? As the exhibition at London's Design Museum demonstrated, Paul Smith's playful attitude to fashion is infectious. Fun is crucial to his world – as is, of course, some of the smartest tailoring around.

JENNA LYONS

Most influential designers work in high fashion, with runway collections and four-figure price tags, but Jenna Lyons (1969–) is an exception. The creative director and president of J.Crew, she has made the preppy retailer – once the go-to for Middle America's basics – a serious fashion contender. In the noughties, a decade when a high-low aesthetic flourished, J.Crew realized that its time was now.

Lyons has a penchant for mixing colours and textures, and juxtaposing sports and precious fabrics, and the start of several trends can be laid at her door. She championed the statement necklace worn with jeans, printed tux-style trousers and the fashion sweatshirt. All about mixing day and night or casual and glamorous, Lyons's hybrids are a perfect solution to how we want to dress now.

Lyons has worked at J.Crew for the entirety of her design career, starting as a junior designer in 1990. Her emergence as a figurehead of the brand came with the arrival of Mickey Drexler the current CEO, in 2004. The two have become a dream team of retail success. J.Crew is now a favourite of the Obamas, and a pit stop for high-fashion consumers who want to add a bit of cut-price cool into their wardrobes. It now has over 300 branches in the United States, stores in London and an estimated worth of nearly $2 billion.

Lyons's own style is no doubt a factor in the brand's success. Her picks on the brand's website are bookmarked by the savvy J.Crew shopper. She embodies the fashion philosophy, mixing their pieces with high-fashion labels for that high-low look. J.Crew's world domination is only just beginning, and Lyons is right at the centre of it.

With classic pointed stilettos, coral lipstick, long glossy mane and those trademark glasses, Jenna Lyons advertises J.Crew style expertly. Little details like the leopard clutch say a lot about the brand philosophy: keep it simple, then add a twist.

INDEX